THE GEORGIA POETRY PRIZE

The University of Georgia Press established the
Georgia Poetry Prize in 2016 in partnership with
the Georgia Institute of Technology, Georgia State
University, and the University of Georgia. The prize
is supported by the Bruce and Georgia McEver Fund
for the Arts and Environment.

WINTER HERE

The University of Georgia Press    *Athens*

# Winter Here

*Poems*

JESSICA TANCK

Published by the University of Georgia Press
Athens, Georgia 30602
www.ugapress.org
© 2024 by Jessica Tanck
All rights reserved
Designed by Erin Kirk
Set in Arno

Most University of Georgia Press titles are
available from popular e-book vendors.

Printed digitally

Library of Congress Control Number: 2023946594
ISBN: 9780820366654 (paperback)
ISBN: 9780820366661 (epub)
ISBN: 9780820366678 (PDF)

*for my mother*

# Contents

( O N E )

## So Below

*I can walk through fire*, I told my mother, drunk
on the glow of sparklers, on sand cooling
in the sunset. I might have been five or six
years old, inflated with the recklessness
and certainty that come from living
in one's imagination. Architect of sandcastles,
tender of flame, I paraded the beach in orange
swimsuit and water shoes, ready for thrill.
There was everything, here: fire and the great
water breathing, moving, cold that stretched
all the way to the horizon. And I felt it,
that bigness. Pictured the sand crumbling
into cakes of earth and rock below us,
how deep the world stretched on every side.
My sister and I, sparklers in hands,
zagged into evening like fireflies or bats,
weightless, moved by joy. And my grandparents
were inside, and my mother and father here
on the beach, and what wasn't protecting
me, what wasn't stretching above, what
didn't comfort me in my smallness? *I can*
*walk through fire*, I told her, and believed it.
Stood at the threshold of glow. Having never
felt the suck and sear of it, having never nursed
a burnt knuckle under cold water or whimpered
for relief from a tongue of flame beneath my skin.
*I can walk through fire*, I said, and my mother sat
still in her seat. Eyes locked in the flames, she said, *No.*
*You can't.* Didn't even look up, did not look at me.

# Morning Sickness

It's true I can't remember ever being hugged by my mother,
but I do recall being led by my dad to her bedside

every morning near the end. My sister and I stood there
in our backpacks and jumpers, lined up as if to offer

something, as if we might reach her wherever she was.
Too small to see much over the piled blankets, I tried

to fit my arms around her as my eyes veered away, darted
at the bedroom window, which looked out at a brick wall—

terrified of being caught forever in her hair, its cobweb
strands draped quiet down the bed, bathed in the smell

of sleep. I cannot remember her as waking or asleep but
somewhere in between, face up in some underworld river.

Even now I wonder at her ever-open, ever-shut eyes, worry
that she is still angry with me for pulling away—for wanting to.

My dad says she used to lock me and my sister in closets.
This, too, I can't remember, but I like to think

it an act of safekeeping—her pressing a kiss
to each of our foreheads, holding us for a moment before

shutting us in. Leaving us to the warm dark, the quiet.
Us two peering through the slats at the lit room beyond—

the kind of light you can only see from a pocket
of darkness. The kind of light into which one must break.

# Damned If

When we left the room, still locked in character
by tartan jumpers and the beetle wings of our Mary
Janes, my sister said the people had been creepy.

Inside, we'd joined a circle of clammy hands
while strangers rocked and shuddered, babbled
in tongues. In the rearview mirror, my father's eyes

hovered. This, he said, was God's native tongue—the language
we needed to get help. But I didn't feel God in that room.
Instead: stir-fried syllables, unfamiliar touch. Voices

untangled from sense, soaking me in a burning
spring. It was a kind of pleasure: mind drowsy, eyes vague
at the blackboard, the slate of night hanging velvet

down the windows. Like a crown of light, this fervor
was almost enough to make you believe in it, a show of force:
ocean smashing up under an edifice of rock.

Absent of meaning, the boom and crash of it was still
enough to shake me, pin me on my back at night, expecting
the floor to open into some deep dark below.

# The Body in Time

### I.

If language forms the world, ours was walled
with pies, robins, bonfires. I can't help thinking
my mind erected a world too vast
to fill in, a kingdom of flames that didn't sear
and adults whose hands swung perpetually
out of reach. I thought little of bodies,
except to delight in the apparent invincibility
of my own. Erased, elided, smoothed.
I draped altars in velvet, populated seas
with monsters sailing deep below ships.

### II.

It is easy to imagine we know others with the body
as touch point—as marker, illusion, or friend.
My grandfather's hands chopping scallions:
his patience, the rocking knife. Fingers that dwarfed
the roots, slow, deliberate no matter the outward clatter,
steam, or sizzle. And after, the piles of green and white
arranged like a buffet on the cutting board. Order
I could see from behind his hunched back.

### III.

On Assateague Island, we watched horses thunder
along the surf, and I plucked a bulb of cactus
as a souvenir. Now, my souvenir is my mother
tweezing needles from my palms and fingers,
the strange suck as each barb left my skin. At
her funeral a year later, when I saw the urn
and asked, bewildered, "Where's her body?"
everyone laughed. But it wasn't funny, was it?

# Circa 1999

I fought a boy at school & was suspended for a week.
A hunk of cardboard, filleted like a whitefish, had flown in
over the chain-links. It lit on the asphalt, a possibility.

Maybe because the playground was bare, a skeleton
of a swing set the only fossil, toy thing. Maybe because
the imagination is ravenous, always wanting

for props. Maybe the cardboard was ragged like owls or sad
suede couches & therefore worthy of trust. I picked it up.
Stroked the soggy pulp of it, its folds of broken wing.

When the boy snatched it from me, I scratched him,
drew blood from his cheek, a beat before he punched me.
A line of red that led to me alone watching my father

feed my animals, the plush friends I slept with,
to a black bag: my plump chicken, smiling bear & dog
all gone, cleared away for my new toy. We lay there together,

the cardboard & I. My face damp & swollen, I eyed its craggy
silhouette, curled away from its corner of the bed. Wished
it gone. Shut my eyes to it, tried to keep it out. Forgot.

Perhaps the dreams came early, a sleep that lasted weeks.
I dreamt of absence, interplay of shadow, a world of sea.
Or perhaps an angel came to get it, cut with light the bars

outside my window, took the ragged thing away from me.
Or a stick against the window hushed its changing,
knocked, concealed some rush & feather whorl & screech.

# Pet Crow

When I find the crow in the bath,
Alesha says the spirits will follow us forever.
The first horror of presence, of dark clotting

the white-washed tub, and I don't even shriek.
Like the time I stepped out of bed onto a sponge
of carpet, a book floating in water the river pushed

through the door cracks, or when I lifted the sheets
to find our pet fish's bones arranged
in a neat little skeleton, a cat's jigsaw,

or when Father gasped tar into toilet bowl,
pins forced in a cross beneath his belly skin
like Houdini's lockpicks,

I don't panic. Father says there's devil
in my calm, but this is not the only crow.
Under the porch, the first one stretched.

The next, broken on the concrete,
a bloody slash on the bedroom window.
Outside—a coincidence. Inside, no.

Alesha brings me a Walmart bag, watches
as I scoop soaked black feathers
into plastic film.

I can feel its bones,
the creature
beneath the symbol.

It would have made a good pet, I think,
and turn the plastic like a shroud over
its gaping beak. We haven't had a pet

in years— not since the cat went mad.
We bring the crow outside, wanting to bury it
somewhere the light won't see.

We want it to be forgiven.

# History of Silence

Those mornings before school my sister & I
    would float through the kitchen, toast bread
in the dark while coffee roiled a storm

    through its purring machine. Every movement careful,
our hands more real when they faltered, tripped
    for a saucer or the long cold of a spoon. Familiar

in worn flannel, we would sit at the table
    & wait together for the little candle of dawn. I'd try
to guess her thoughts in the color of that silence,

    to parse them in the fist curled to her mouth, the gleam
of her eyes. Unable to speak, unwilling to face the night
    spilling from under my bedroom's lockless door, I'd follow

her eyes: pine out the windows, evergreens shuddering
    beyond the glass where ice carved its continents,
maps of fracture that soon glowed backlit by sun.

## Courtesy and Horror

*after Sharon Olds*

To be clean was to be good, and vice versa.

Every baseboard, tile, and mirror spotless,

the deserts of white carpet and linoleum

a proof we weekly scrubbed blank.

My sister and I laughing through fogs

of ammonia as we scrubbed the kitchen floor,

bandanas hugging our faces like hospital

gowns. Cleanliness meant innocent meant

nothing to hide. Supplicant

to a higher order, white-touched and still

as the doe when the arrow enters.

When a coworker scrawled #1 BITCII ♡

on my forearm in Sharpie, I lingered

in the dark back room after our shift

and took steel wool to the skin until

both it and ink were stripped. A good thing,

a clean thing—did the difference matter?

The filthy ate the clean.

## Unseen Current, Livid Hand

Dear reader, I'm afraid
this is a ghost story.

*

My parents were teenagers the first time
they touched a Ouija board.

Read the name the shadow spelled
out with their hands and jumped

when a glass vase flung itself
across the room,

shattered against the wall.
The incision made.

A door opened.

*

A generation later, it writhed
back to life when my stepbrother

emptied the hairs from dad's razor
into a plastic bag. We found

the little altar in his apartment,
the snake. *A spell of separation,*

we were told. Our house chilled
to freezing. Pictures vanished

from their frames and stone crosses fell
from walls. Our pets, especially,

seemed in peril: gone from their cages,
found bloodied or wandering

in the dark. My hamster went missing
for hours before I found her in the lining

of my backpack, pawing,
the seams still intact.

My father sickened.

\*

Pins in his belly,
vomiting black.

What hand stuck the pins,
scratched the wedding pictures

from their frames, carved
the Cross of Saint Peter

into fabric, flesh, and wall?
What hand carried the bodies

of our hamsters, lifted
the fish's bones, the dead crow?

\*

Once we moved, it faded
gradually, though it could

be set off by a call, a letter
from my stepbrother, or by nothing

at all. Missing figurines, a broken platter.
Pennies in threes under the rugs.

They found the shattered cake platter
filthy in a cupboard, my sister's missing

homework torn and rust-stained
underneath my bed. *Did you do this?*

My father, livid, the papers in his hands.
No, I said.

Why would spirits do this?

I hadn't. Or I didn't remember
if I had. They found matching stains

on my pajamas, assigned two motives:
*jealousy* and *spite*. Days earlier,

I'd pulled one of my mother's old books
on the occult off the shelf. Read a chapter

on mind control
before pushing it back, feeling chilled.

Did I do it, reader?

*

I became afraid
of what might use my body

while I slept. Had I erased
the photos, twisted the frames

and crosses, hurt my pets?

*

My father installed video cameras
throughout the house, sandwiched

tape recorders under furniture,
behind bookshelves. He was worried

about my gaps in memory.
*You may be losing time*, he said.

\*

A decade later, I don't trust myself
to open the right book.

Still retreat from crevices and corners,
anywhere large and dark enough

to hide a body. I avoid the spine
of anything too hungry, eyes

on my feet, my mouth shut.
Afraid that if I reach for answers,

it will meet me in the mirror
at the end of some long hallway,

light a place that ought
be left to wither—

turn me over
in the dark.

# Eating Flamin' Hot Cheetos at Mom's Grave

Scarlet feathered orange, neon yellow, the flames
on the bag make burning look fun. It's hard to tell
if Chester's overcome by the fire—his shades hide
his eyes, his smile a kind of jawless flame-gasp,
perpetual. The tree above drips ice on my shoulder,
weepier than me. Kicked out again, I wear my goth
sensibility like a wool coat. I can just feel the snow
through my jeans, the cold an epic poem, a thing
I live in. World still unlit, no phone or laptop, this
is my place to go. Me and Mom and her stone.
LOVING MOTHER AND WIFE. The etching's
full of grit, dirt-packed. I crunch a Cheeto, mull
its salty pulp. I am not sure about these terms.
My hand red raw, I crumple it back in the bag,
warm it, fish for more. I can't picture her face
anymore, just a specter, back turned. Linen-rot
and lilies. Her angry intellect clutched like a blade
she couldn't swing without slicing open her own
palms. Bag empty, I suck the red from my fingers,
plunge a hand in the pocket of my coat. When I
asked if she was dying, she cried, shook her head no.
I tried, is what I tell myself. I wonder if she'd agree,
what she'd have scrawled if she'd left a note.
The snowy hills and their gray tangle of trees don't
say a word. Kneeling in the dim, winter stretches on
unmovable, pristine. Pen out, I scrape the etching clean.

( T W O )

# Samson et Dalila, Op. 47

I would wonder over it often: the welt
on my teacher's throat. My hand cupped
round the neck of my cello, hollow

I hugged to me. So thin the music
stand, so thin what kept the din of strings
from the electric weather

of my blood. In profile my teacher's
tucked hair, frown, perpetual bruise.
Horsehair on metal, purr torn from a gate

thrown open—and to what?
Only when she lifted her violin to play
would I understand the mark—

how close she held the carved thing
to tear its music out.

# Litany of Priests

The first was Father Mayer, of the brocaded stoles and bald head. His face almost featureless from afar.

Father Glenn, my favorite, grayed at the temples. His high, soft voice singing as he blessed our house, sprinkling water on the shadows. How he crouched to speak with me, to ask the questions hand on shoulder, eye to eye.

Fathers at the pulpit, within the carved confessional. Fathers at the chalkboard, on the playground, in the hall. Robed in gowns or sweater-vests or flannel. Music from the throat or speakers, from the organ climbing up the hallowed walls.

Mr. R, with the big voice, who loved Mark Twain. Mr. M, who taught me the precision and purity of chess.

K, who taught the dismal science. Loved medieval music. Knelt on ice to help me fill the January-withered tires of my car.

C, who read me the scene where he went back and killed his father. Almost smiling as the sun slipped from the windows, desks circled under the fluorescent lights.

Father seething, driving wolves out of the temple. Father stripping ornament from writing, wood, and walls.

Father longing, marked and maker. Priest of poems and broken bones.

Father, though the house is burning.

Father, bound in flesh, who holds the structure up.

## Poem with Failed Blood Sacrifice

I've always liked the world
lit by fire, cast in Old Testament law.

It meant someone else had to see me—
burn away my wrongs.

For a long time, it worked that way:
my face, the wet hay, how I hurt after.

I'm a liar for claiming this will ever be enough—
even as my spine palms the wall and I twist,

ride the shiver, stroke the dark
hair back from your eyes—my mind

tugs me, a chain pulled taut. Good as gone,
desire brittle as a lightning-struck tree.

Begging the question of how alive
a trapped thing can be.

In the dim barn mirror, I watch my fingers
comb blood from my hair—

and tremble with the thrill of cleansing.

# Overture in D♭ Minor

Glass, because it was irregular, the smashed lip
　　of the Coke bottle
　like a calligraphy pen.

Because in their disorder, those sketched lines
　　could be confused
　for a slip of the hand.

*

Hand that rocked vibrato, thumb
　　and finger, hand which made a hinge
that let the low notes purr and sing.

Fingers pressed and plucked the steel,
　　with flesh unlocked the music, tore the skin
and built it to be harder, eyes locked

on the conductor's hands. Crescendo,
　　scent of varnish. You become
a sea of moving arms, a lung.

*

Glass, yes, because it lacked
　　precision, seemed less cruel, without
the surgical geometry of blade—the marks

like gills cut into my lab partner's forearm,
　　which I saw but never acknowledged. Which
everyone saw before they turned and looked away.

# Judge Claude Frollo Finds the Child a New Home

*He was a priest, austere, grave, morose; one charged with souls.*
—Victor Hugo, *Notre-Dame de Paris*


Remember the leather chair, the window
behind the desk against which light pressed

its hands and watched? How it haloed
him, backlit, washed the mouth, nose,

the very eyes from his face. It didn't let you
take shelter, that light—instead opened

onto your eyes and shoulders, lips, lap.
How small you must've looked

under that grand ceiling,
peeled open by the afternoon

sun. See your hands damp and twisted,
hair unkempt: child talking with the shadow

of a man, petitioning the wrong god
for help, kneeling in the fireplace to pray.

# Nowhere, WI

Nothing ever moved in that house.

Even the puppy, which first sniffed the kitchen frenetic as a bird heart, melted into a puddle on the stairs. A pool of black-and-white with eyes too dark to read.

The neon stillness of a digital clock.

Contrary to the witness statement, nothing happened there.

Only the stone frog burbling water from the pond outside.

May the record show that the windows were open always, even when the pond froze solid, as February licked ice down her spine. No light ever cut on after dusk.

We submit that it is impossible to view footage from cameras I, V, and X due to this murk. Not even the pond can be questioned, as it, too, has ambered in the pine cones' rot.

The algae-choked gurgle of water.

Night after night. How it pushed voices below it. The sole testimony, until the water froze.

What sound the ice would make when struck.

# Elsewhere

I am trying to pay attention but can't hear over it.
The cold humming through the hairline fracture
in my jaw. It's a song like white noise, crackling
a throb down the spine of all I want, feel, or touch.
*You look tired.* It's our usual walk, along the crown
of his property line, boots slipping in the mud
that tunnels, breaks open the forest below. My hair
whips and freezes in the wind, and I think how clean
I'd be with ice in my skin. I imagine it like a tongue
of flame, the shock and sear of it—and I must nod,
because there's his hand in my hair. He pulls me
to him as if holding me hard enough will call me back.
*You seem to be elsewhere.* His breath. Lips, the rasp of stubble
against my ear. *I'm sorry.* I go still. Over his shoulder,
there's a doe nuzzling, gaunt, through the thicket below.
Ribs jut her flank. Ears spread trembling.
How to tell him the world's under water—that all
that's real is the damp cuff of my flannel, distant geese.

# St. Teresa's School for Haunted Girls

The nightmares are terrible.

You rock rabbits in your arms. Their eyes scream in frequency with yours.

If the rifles weren't chained in the shed for incurables—

*

Most of the teachers are men, which makes them fathers or gods. Wrathful, cloaked.

*

Shocks don't force the memories to surface. You rattle, say you don't want to know. Better to wake rust-soaked and wonder.

*

Nobody will confirm whether it was a dream, a ghost, or a devil.

They bandage your arms, leave you curled on the paper bed.

You mistake footsteps for thunder.

# While We Slept

Frost inside the single-pane window,
walls that shivered against wind.
I'd never thought about climate control
until I didn't have it, perched on a hill
above Lyttelton Harbour where the water
ran cold for an hour after a toilet flush.
Outside, water spat ice on my neck
and soaked the leggings beneath my jeans.
No central heating and you start to get
*Jane Eyre* on a visceral level; I used to
wonder why they bothered with common
rooms until I lived it, realized the cold
herds you to wherever there's heat. Once
we lit a fire in the woodstove and a bird
screamed out, tangled itself in the curtains
as it sought shelter. Cold woke me up, kept
me painfully aware, made me tremble in
showers. The worst part: tremors in the teeth
and hands, bitter air, hair becoming ice.
On the far side of the earth, thirteen hours
hurtling across shadowy ocean, what liberated me
also terrified. Far enough away to forget
my own name, to harden and fang
into a survivor. When I looked up
at the hills that crowned the village, spikes
of evergreens, it was easy to imagine my wolf
life. In reality, though, I sought comfort,
as a coward does. I lied. Earlier, I lied. Worse
than cold air, drip of water, my blue-tinged
fingers—was curling myself to my partner,
who'd been made strange, displaced and sunk,
while I stared open-eyed into the dark. No
wolf after all, but alone nonetheless. How'd
I arrive here, I'd wonder. Nothing but ocean
in sight, lightless water forever, the only boat.

# Elysium

Everything is cold here somehow, the blue of evening
    sunk in winter. The violets come

in three flavors: original, yellow, and white. You saw
    your old friend, her lungs clear of tar, and she sang to you.

They'd stitched her back together,
    but she was colder, too, violets limp in her palms.

Everything from before—noise, orange, buffalo chicken pizza—
    it all reads as reconstructed memory. Echo, almost,

because the anodyne filter here blocks out pain: heat and want
    damp, gone to seed. In this half-blank world, have you been

erased? Are you new? No, the air here is too comfortable for that.
    All breeze, no wind. It almost makes you miss the cruelty

of winter—immense black sky caked on livid white,
    a Caravaggio toppled in shadow,

which could be the trick of an eye, a dream, a recurring
    wonderland or nightmare—

but a passing truck threw wet across your face and you knew.
    Stung with certainty that this—this part—was real.

# Fire and Powder

We trudged drunk into the blizzard
outside. Were unable to resist
its gathering quiet, armed
with a thermosful of red wine.

Had fed and fed the fire
until the hearthstone seared
our hands. The burning
an invitation. An occasion.

Our intent: the overpass.
To watch the plows eat
highway snow from our perch
in the whited night.

These were the nights
cold echoed, when it seemed
anything I didn't spend
would slip off in the dark.

Snow spiraled, so deep,
and we'd gone a mile
before I reached in my pocket,
didn't feel the key. Turned, split off.

I woke in that otherworld, pulled
up by her hands, in a snowbank
splashed burgundy. Had drifted
off with a tongue of warmth
that I fail and fail to keep.

# Pedagogy

Learn it wrong the first time
and it'll be a bitch to rewrite—

a broken finger healed crooked
or the livid scar you tug sleeve over
for the rest of your life.

Q: Is learning more a function of
teacher or student?

Of lesson plan or the slab of brain
who takes the test?

While prepping for the GRE, I choked
for months on the word "hackneyed."

No matter what I did, a bile-flavored memory
rose each time I saw it:

I was eight when my father found a snake
nuzzling through the mulch in our yard.

He caught it in his gloved hands, stalked
into the shed, and emerged with a hatchet.

I watched as he hacked it in seven, every line
broken except the bright stripe on its back.

Discuss: What was my father's
teaching method?

But I watched, didn't I.

When I was seventeen, I learned what
a digital artery was with my hand cupped full of red,

pale with the terror of sloshing blood on the cream carpet.
How we tend to know only the names of what's broken—

learn our bones', muscles', veins' merit through harm.


                      Q: How much does desire
             to learn, an abiding interest, pull the cart?

                  Can you learn from this poem
         if we don't have the same severed parts?

# Singularity at Ninety Mile Beach

The Tasman Sea has no regard for our pain,
we discover sobbing for breath postriptide.

Buoyed by salt water, we'd drifted further out,
cuts singing in ocean while our scalps fried

in the sun. Since to be embodied is to repeat the past,
haunt the halls where we've hurt, I was happy to drown

in the sea's feast. I simmered in utter distraction,
dizzy on it. Eventually, the shore yawned at us,

and we blinked back: two specks of person in the vast
blue. On the sand after, breathless and brined, I see where

the riptide dragged you over rock, your knee bleeding
in the sand. Our panic-drunk laughter, my hand on your face

asking if I might borrow you for awhile.
Your hair drips, skin warm, and I wonder

whether this is my only way to really know you:
through the wall of your skin. Each of us caught

for the moment, held here and forced
to be present as a pair of cracked ribs.

# Charleston, NZ

Bull kelp thrashed to shore
looking so animal from afar
I had to sidestep the surge
of white water to touch it,
wonder at the car tire
tentacles, unbroken and full
of air. A small, angry beach,
the gray of which stuck in
my throat even as the wind
ripped my hair, dragged
water past rock to the hairline
of cold jungle. Everywhere
the abandoned coal mines
and the specters of towns
that followed them
to the end like starving
horses. Outside one
mine, rust and cobwebs
guarded an honesty
box, a sign that warned:
*Bring your own light.* Down
through the carved door,
the air was a hand
that closed over
my mouth.
The walls floated up
to meet us, sand
and buried tunnels
in the cell-phone
flashlight,
pockets of
a vein just
aching to
shut.

( T H R E E )

# Sanctuary

What I loved best was to play angry.
Grind the bow deep in metal, rewrite

my prints against string and fingerboard.
Rage and savor-sing. To break fortissimo.

And after, to stroke the loosened strands
of horsehair. To rip them from the bow.

\*

There was the lapping water, shore arcing away
from the power plant's shadow, its churn and red-

light blink. Crumbled concrete, rusted nails of old jetties.
Waves came and went, forever cold on my bare feet.

Sunset washed the wet sand incandescent,
made the thorns and sawgrass impossible to see.

\*

And the long, dusty corridors of my school.
Wide stairwells, bulletin boards, far

corners lit by the vending machines' glow.
We walked a tunnel to the church. Close

ceilings, freckled tile on the floors. A hum
when we filed through, our heads bowed low.

\*

When the migraines came, or flu, or hurt,
I knew I would be safe. In this way, I learned

to take care: with lemon and honey bright
in green tea, steaming ginger, echinacea. With bears

holding GET WELL signs and the little bottles
of Lourdes water tipped into my throat. With alcohol

swabs and Bacitracin, gauze and bandages, with wounds
cleaned and dressed neatly, with perfect tenderness.

How better to love one another?

\*

Those hidden places beneath the evergreens:
ocher worlds of pine needles, branches sheltering

the sharp forest floor. How winter would consecrate
those trees, make them go quiet with snow.

\*

The dream goes like this: a normal day,
always someone I know, a person I love,

at the wheel. I never expect the car
to accelerate wildly. To be pressed to the seat

by velocity. *Where are you going?* I always wonder.
Until we peel over the side of some great bridge

to nowhere, sail over the guardrail
into the deep below.

# Darknet Classifieds

1

Widowed father of four seeking governess
for children aged 2–19. Payment in orchids.
Clothing provided upon arrival at residence.

2

Wanted: mind reader with a high tolerance
for pain. Expect glass on the floor (30 years'
marriage). Pay dependent upon experience.

3

Ambitious, attractive tutor ready to fill your
vacancies. Learn to hate sans remorse,
to quiet the tremors in your hands and teeth.

4

Gentle companion needed for baking and
recreational psychedelics use. Clean shaven,
no lung problems. Sense of humor a must.

5

FOR SALE: adolescent white egret, one
mangled wing. Good poolside companion
and/or daughter for the terminally alone.

6

Seeking in-home cellist to be my personal songbird.
Mansion full of shade and tropical plants. Grieving
experience essential. Do not bring furniture.

# Phone Call with My Sister, 2018

The walls sink back into dark, the cats
orange and gray gargoyles at the window,

so quiet they would disappear
if I just shut my eyes.

But before: no music but lawn mower
and smoke through the open screen door.

Why collect these stacks of postcards,
books, stolen feathers, and leaves?

To nest our past, grip it in house. Tang
of grass stings through the buttery oboe

that floats from the building next door: cracked
alley of shattered glass and fire ants. Caesura

strung with weighted power lines, guarded by
the beady panic of squirrels. Everywhere dusk

empties against the windows, forced in by train song,
the horn low and long over the hunched city.

Crickets break the drone, insist, creak. Jungle air,
perfect conduit for lightning bugs and longing. No—

it will never feel more solid than this, the warm
cinderblocks and the voice that crackles tin in my ear.

# Home-wrecker

One grad-school Sunday,
        a shattering: the woman's voice
wavers outside my open window,

too near below. *This is what you do?*
        Thick, liquid voice—
*you're going to use me like this?*

    —the sort of unspeakable
        from which we cower, turn away.
Until the glass breaks: shatters, unmade.

*

There is what you can witness and then
        the current underneath. Laughter
through the floorboards. A touch *(like this?)*

of hands, eyes locked at a party. A kiss
        on the curbside while cicadas sing beneath.
Times when *(this is what you do?)*

judgment seems to nod, to sleep. Gestures
        that depend on the one who makes
them. Depend on who reads them, sees.

*

But that first stab of longing. First
        gasp, first charge and blood rush,
stammer of ecstatic tongue.

Every text, pint, walk home
        in the winter,
every look recast in light and shame.

For desire, too, is inconsolable. No one
         can tell you: here is what you will
be given, and this is what it will take.


\*


The day my mother died, we didn't go
         to school, but to my babysitter's
place. Cereal, clean white carpets.

I knew nothing, didn't get what it meant
         when they said my mother, thirty-five, *had died
in her sleep*. But I felt safe up high in that apartment,

with its sun, its plants and smooth glass table.
         I touched the curtains. Out those windows,
there was so much light, but nothing you could really see.

# What We Keep

We've always had some form of shelter,
safety: good boots, fat McIntosh apples

from my grandparents, the angel I'd imagine folded
round me while I slept. White dunes:

sugar melting the strawberries' jeweled mess
to jam. Most years of my childhood

there was a cafeteria with rectangle pizza and the roar
of talk as interlude between silences, a friend's voice

crackling through the plastic landline, distant but real.
There has always been a school, the smell of pencils

and dusty hallways, a teacher sitting with me under
the fluorescent lights and after, always a Perkins

or Denny's, a friend's room piled with blankets,
rain in the streetlight from the warm cabin

of a parked car. I have fled to affection in every form
I can get it: heart emoji or hand cupped to my knee,

the whiskered attention of my cats, who see only what's in
the room. But even now, every time you touch me, I hope

I'm somehow becoming less myself. As if you might draw me
out like water from a lung—leave the ghost, start new.

# Burnt Offering

I'm sorry for papering my fridge with every note
you've ever left me, for how I pin them like evidence
on a conspiracy board. Sorry for how I crane my neck
to watch your eyes instead of the show. Forgive me
my fear, for how my voice and I falter when you
walk through my door. It's just that I am still learning
how this world of yours works. It's that love
as I learned it was a physics of violence, or maybe
alchemy is a better word. I had my shoddy rituals:
lilies, caramel truffles, and handmade birthday cards
I would lay like apologies on the counter. Hugs
offered from thresholds, scribbled-out jokes.
But the problem with such rituals, as with any
summoning: you never know what might show up
and when it might go. One night, mai tais
with hard laughter, dirty jokes on the kitchen floor;
the next, a cold light cut on at midnight, *you'll be sorry*
in the morning as I tugged the door closed.
How to say that memory is a problem for me,
but so is forgetting—that I can be like a rabbit
numb to time, to clover, to water and cloves, having
shivered off everything but the hunger of wolves.
See? Even here: more fucking wolves. I used to worry
no matter what soft breeze turned or how sweet the fire
stirred with song, part of me, like Isaac, might always be
bound, bleating, on a stone—eyes fixed on a raised
and trembling hand, now gone. But your hands
cradling the cat as you carry him to the window
to watch the birds. Your hands careful against
a pineapple's spiny bark. Or stirring circles through
my hair, combing the nightmares out. Your hands a proof
I've been too afraid to put to words, the way
I've only ever been able to pray in the dark, alone.

# Not Crying in Union Station

*Chicago, IL*

It is September and I miss my dead mother,
my sick father, the hand that once held mine,
led me through these halls. Even when we traveled
together, there was always the fear
of splintering off. The terror of being unable
to return home, to warm baths and pajamas,
voices from every floor, the blood of familiars
you knew you would find in every room—perish
the thought of being kept from comfort, being
kept from keeper-from-harm.

Now there is the timetable,
the queue, the attendant leading me and my family
of strangers out of the Hall. Our line loosens, falls
apart as we march ever faster through. Queued
up at the tracks, I hear automated voices burble over
each other, stutter out staggered track names.
Do I know where I'm going? *Track number nineteen.*
*Track number sixteen. Track number thirty-one.* As if
all these places, all these ages, were happening
at once. *Track number seven. Track number twenty-one.*
*Track number twenty-five.* Do I remember the way back?

Somewhere my five-year-old alter wanders
a department store, travels a maze of glass
and clothes racks, looking for my mother's coat—
knocking on all the mirrors trying to let her out.

## Damnatio memoriae

I am the mongrel in the rectory,
glutted on bread and blood.

Some days I wander back
to the pews, sit and rattle

in the varnished shadows. I pray
at the thing that hangs above me,

the thing listening in my tank of dark.

I stare at where it would be
until my eyes gum shut.

For an epoch, no one comes.

More rocking, more creaking,
the smell of wet pine bark.

My eyes, like the windows,
have dimmed in the murk.

What makes a window not a hole?

Something to see, a world on either side.
This is no world. Not anymore.

It is a wound. A wet thing
made only out of mouth.

# Darknet Product/Service Reviews

1

Not worth the time unless you're
so thirsty your throat's stripped.
Stay home and take the pills instead.

2

Sweet girl. But usually waist-deep
in lake, dodging the gnarled fingers
of low-hanging branches and/or men.

3

Disappointed. Within days of staining,
both the wood in question and adjacent
bedrooms were crawling with centipedes.

4

Eroticism of the highest order. Hairless,
concave beauty. Pray that I'll be forgiven.

5

The scent of this dip haunts my dreams.
Will never be able to look my brother
in the face again. Use with caution.

6

Makes me feel loved. Barely need human touch
with a chair this supportive. Like sinking
beneath the silt of a lake full of midnight.

7

Do note that if submerged beyond six hours,
body hair will fry off. If stench and/or inner
ear pain persists after two uses, call for assistance.


8

Mostly innocuous, but cut
with a copper edge you'll gash
your tongue on. Savor it.

# Key Lime Pie

For once, I am looking forward.

To squeezed limes crowding the counter
in a room more wooded stone
than cinderblock and linoleum.

To a bright place. The music inconsequential
but floating nearby—doing its part to carry
the current of the day.

I'll sing my nonsense, crack the eggs,
mix the whole thing still and quiet as cream.
Knowing deep water is just a drive away.

Unfortunately, there will be pollen.
And, of course, dust. Wasps to be fought off
with sneakers and laminated books.

But your arms will enfold me
before I can even chill the pie.
Closed eyes, the smell of sun-warm

grass, your hands still a synonym
for tender. I will probably laugh
in my shock.

What a wonder it'll be to be
surprised by you even then.
So much a wonder

I may even let slip the whole mess.

# Hospitality

*Gracious* is the word we were armed with.
To be flawless barometers of thirst. Hands

folded behind our backs, to see and give
no more or less than what was desired.

A kind of absence in presence, so dressed
in reverence and quiet that one might forget

it was labor to begin with. Perfect work
for one who wanted to button herself up

in devotion—the kind of profession
into which you can simply disappear.

# Gift of the Magi

You are with me in the McDonald's
this time, and I am still the saddest

person here. Your gaze
a hard line at the far wall.

I can feel it gather
in you like a blood clot,

a cyclone—first chill of storm, first gust
dragging rain through the street. How quiet

you get when I am quiet, how soon
your hand drops away from mine.

How dark the village goes
when I cannot get my lamp to light.

Sometimes I want to be touched
when I am blank. Instead, *How are you?*

I ask, and get: *You are clearly
incredibly upset.* And I have been,

for three days, but backtrack,
obfuscate, apologize.

What does honesty matter?

We are both liars: me with my well
of calm, you with the work that keeps you

from nights, from dinner, and now
lunch. We hear our number called,

and you walk up, ask for a second bag, start
to divide the food. I think of what my dad said

about my mother's last year of life:
how exhausting it became, hearing

her talk of suicide. How it was almost a relief
when she finally succeeded, a dread lifted

from the kitchen drawers, the dresser,
bathtub, every hard stair. *I am sorry.*

Your hands play soft Tetris, move the last
of the sandwiches into the second bag,

the paper bright. We walk together
and I laugh with you at the pizza parlor being

ridden by a bulldozer, call it divine comeuppance
for the sauceless buffalo chicken pizza

they sent us a month ago—the three-hour
wait for it, my notorious bad luck. I laugh,

apologize again, kiss you goodbye
at the intersection where we always split.

*Thank you for the wonderful morning,*
I hear myself say before you cross, before

I start my walk home, paper cup
of Diet Coke cold in my hand. I am giving

you a gift. I am giving you a gift
I do not know how to take back.

( F O U R )

# Ode to Wisconsin

Come home, beloved. To precipice and shadow.
To tangled woods flying past. To wind that stirs

the spirits in these carved hills, makes dance
the Northwoods evergreens, rustles them in gust.

Your loneliness is no pathology. How else to feel,
with the sky hung so close, the heavens peeled

raw? How else could you take the open sky, the dark,
save for the cold, pockmarked moon gauzed in clouds,

the shards of northern lights? This place, halfway between
Earth and the stars. Past pastures and rotted barns, woodsmoke

and taverns, fens where even the devil cries himself to sleep.
Dead leaves steeped in amber water, the damp firebrand

of fall. And always the lakes, designed to draw the eye
and lure us silent to their cold and depth, the force

of their whitecaps. Soften our voices, curl our vowels
along the tongue. O the brilliance of a bonfire against

vast night. O the warmth of a garage, balm of lamplight
after the drive—salt-bleached tires, your hands

white-knuckling the wheel as your eyes comb shadows
for whitetails who wait to charge the chapel of a midnight road.

## Erebus and Terror

On the phone the night before his surgery,
I try to explain to my grandfather

my obsession with the Arctic,
Franklin's failed expedition.

Five months without sunrise,
the compass swimming circles.

Night after night, frozen in, the groan
of ice against both ships,

hungry and climbing.
Like most things worth fearing,

it was invisible, the danger,
at least to their eyes. *Ineffable,*

my grandfather says, when I struggle
to explain the great white nothing,

how it feels so close, attached to the raw air
back home. *Something you can't put to words,*

he says, and I argue that's why I need to try.
*Are you okay?* he'd asked, minutes earlier,

when I went quiet at his description
of how they'll scrape the cancer out

tomorrow, run the tests. Silence—
sacred punctuation that catches what's true

in its hollows, in the expanse between
our ever-softer repetitions

of *I love you* and *good night.*

## The Axe and the Poplar

Home is this stretch of shore
with the glass house near where

they found the body of my teacher
and the storm-struck poplar now hanging

like a broken finger, crown buried
in the ebb and pull of lake.

*

It's my sister with an axe
in hand, barefoot

on the rocky shore,
flipping back her hair

and grinning as she calls
blade to trunk.

*

There are moments where I see her going
elsewhere, when it's still or sleepy and her eyes

go glassy, lips flat, and I feel that tug
within me, wonder if we see the same

absence. Whether the same thing
is coming home to claim us both.

*

My sister saws through what the axe can't,
flinches to avoid the spray of wood flakes,

and after an hour of hacking finally breaks
through the last inch. The tree is heavy,

lodged in shoreline, so I wade out
into the water, the waves waist-level.

Two steps before the lake climbs
higher, swirls the cotton of my dress,

turns cold where the depths reach up,
and puts my legs to static sleep.

Sand swallows my feet, and I sink deeper
as I join her, strain to grip the holds

of slimy branches, to lift and roll
the trunk across those jagged rocks.

# Waltz No. 2

*after Shostakovich*

It is a sick carnival, carousel tilting into the sea.
Tender-footed percussion in the air, the horns
that might be birdsong, engine, trill of ink.

Singing, how the woodwinds tease. Cursive
and bittersweet. Swell and spin into shadow, into loss
that shuts the eyes, swings and carries feet. Can you see

the grandeur of the curtains, feel the moonlight
cutting through clouds, tent, and ballroom to touch
the cheek? Cupped hand, gesture that tears and leaves.

Dance turns, deep in the brass, slides into golden
bleat. Dark finery. Sardonic laughter, lips snarled just
so. Under enchantment—bloodred mouth, sharp teeth.

# Exploding Suitcase

Open, the floor strewn with discard—
socks, striped blouses, leather jacket

still smelling of storm drain. Return, sure,
unlocks its jaws: delivers one disorder

from another. Stumbles through the airport,
white noise in my calves and feet. Bound

shoulder and thigh, plastic-etched. Taut denim
and blood heat of the woman beside me,

halfway in my seat. This becomes
an exhaustion that stutters, knocks

knees against desks, lets dishes pile
in the sink. The cats' little talons accumulate

on the carpet, in the couch blanketed in fleece.
Anywhere I sit, stand, a small sharp thing waits.

# Winter Here

is inseparable from
my hand in your pocket.

Wind down the collar,
at my throat. The cement streets,

basted in salt, rasp
against my boots. November

opens like a knife, and I can't
stop waiting to hear your footsteps

on the stairs,
to see your shadow through

the frosted glass. The first night
you sent me a poem, Chicago froze

solid. Blood in the merlot
the way I bit my lip. Season

of evening, season of fairy lights,
pomegranates, wool, and ice.

I spent weeks suspended across state lines
with you, our messages a fervor

as the temperature dropped to twenty, forty below.
*Look at how cold,* I said, sent a photo

of my bedroom window turned meat freezer,
the metal frame feathered with frost.

I'd been thrown from a draft horse
on Christmas Eve and texted you pictures

of the bruises as they darkened,
arranged myself, shivering, in flannel—

in candlelight, a smirk and black lace.
It was snowing when you finally arrived

at my door. I could never believe it.
How my hands shook, pulse raced,

mind gone black and blue. How
I undressed in uncertainty, almost afraid

to look at you. Remind me
how lucky I was to wait

and fear in the freezing
quiet, the snow-sunk city.

Tell me: what is reverence
but terror, really—wondering

what the cold hands you've anointed
with your mouth will do.

# Darknet Missed Connections

### 1

You drove a blue mattress truck up
through the pines. I watched from under
the fence. Hard to say hello
through a mouthful of bees.

### 2

A Ouija board might be more useful,
but here goes: your name is carved
in the cello I bought. I can smell
you in the wood, feel you reclining
between my thighs.

### 3

You were standing where
the ocean took the first highway.
Beside the pickled onions and bone
truck. Your eyes ran glacial
down me. I couldn't stop staring
at your bare foot clutching
the gravel on the road's shoulder.

4

Since you stumbled by,
the nails have been weeping
rust down the concrete.
I've seen a fox
lapping at their dirty veins—


5

That urn you overturned?
Well, my sister's
ashes somehow liquefied,
and she's seeping
indigo into the floorboards.
I'll give back your jacket
if you join us
for one last sleepover.


6

I sat for three hours
with its warm neck
in my lap. You liar.
If anything, the clumps
of knotted mane softened me.
Beauty like that—monstrous.

# Long Division

We have split the phone plan,
emptied the safety deposit box.

My dad is moving out of the house:
gone, the sentinel from his office

in the basement, plastic Star Wars
figurines tipped into a box.

It is hard not to imagine all of us
in our old places, hard not to fill

the house with past. Alesha (*sister*,
I still think, not *ex, ex-step*)

cross-legged on the futon, remote
in hand, a bowl of macaroni

in her lap. She peels home
on repeat, inside in a jangle

of keys, stays up with me all night,
perpetually lights and leaves.

Myranda (blood sister) half-absent
in her aerie moves from floor to desk,

floor to desk. My stepmom flickers
in the dark bedroom, in the mirrors,

on the stairs, in the corners of halls.
I am always underneath all of this,

in the skin of the basement or crossing
the yard. How many times do I tread that

bed of needles, climb to the freshly sawn-off
branches, wish a kinder mending, wish

an absence gone? Press my hands to trace
the drip of sap, what cannot be divided,

to touch what bubbles forth, what empties,
amber, from the knotted heart.

# Venichka

"How am I not to be boring and how am I not to drink Kubanskaya?
I've earned the right. I know . . . that 'world sorrow' is not a fiction
perpetrated by the old writers, because I carry it within myself and
know what it is and I do not wish to hide this fact. One must get
used to speaking of one's virtues bravely, to people's faces."
—Venedikt Erofeev, *Moscow to the End of the Line*

From bench to ditch to station to train,
then bench to ditch and back. The carriages

swell and shudder, tremble in the dark. Vinyl seats,
eyes stung by the ceiling lights. To lie, to sleep

with his boots hanging off the seat. Jars of liquor, clear
or stained, and he hears the angels of the Lord. One gram

of vodka per kilometer for the ticket inspector, more
for the aching head, trembling heart. Spirits

and furniture polish. Potion of perfume, foot powder, beer,
and varnish. Black windows wake to burning swallows,

and soon roars of laughter, Koltsov or Ahkmatova recited,
swaying. A drink at every stumble of the tongue. What part

of this is sickness, and what part the soul's design? Divine
inspiration or delirium. Notebooks filled in concrete corners,

fever, thrill, a shot for every page. All the while, woolen hats,
the frigid streets. Sometimes, sleep beneath a grand piano,

wrapped in his coat. I didn't have to imagine the hard floor,
scarce heat. Reader, I admit it was his sorrow that first caught

me. His eyes brimming and glassy, alone in a crowded room,
head starting to swim and fall. Venya, I cannot hear the singer

at the piano either. Venya, I feel cold in my coat. Yet somewhere
the jasmine must be blooming. Somewhere, the birdsong won't stop.

# Acknowledgments

Many thanks to the editors of the following journals, where these poems first appeared, sometimes in slightly different forms:

*The Adroit Journal:* "Eating Flamin' Hot Cheetos at Mom's Grave"

*Beloit Poetry Journal:* "So Below"

*Blackbird:* "Courtesy and Horror" and "Damned If"

*Cincinnati Review:* "Samson et Dalila, Op. 47" and "Gift of the Magi"

*Colorado Review:* "Ode to Wisconsin"

*Cream City Review:* "Darknet Classifieds"

*DIAGRAM:* "Darknet Missed Connections" and "Darknet Product/Service Reviews"

*The Los Angeles Review:* "Morning Sickness"

*Meridian:* "Elysium"

*New Ohio Review:* "Long Division"

Deep gratitude to Travis Wayne Denton, Beth Snead, Jon Davies, Elizabeth Adams, Steven Wallace, Jason Bennett, Christina Cotter, Melissa Gamble, Katie Chaple, Michael Diebert, and everyone at UGA Press. Thank you so much for believing in this book, for helping me bring it to readers—for everything.

Profound thanks to the writing communities of Champaign-Urbana, Madison, and Salt Lake City.

To Chekwube Danladi, Katrina Gaffney, Sybil Mahone, s. g. maldonado-vélez, Ben Miller, Nick Molbert, Cole Piedimonte, Erich Slimak, Aumaine Rose Smith, and every other person at UIUC who shared their brilliance, generosity, and warmth with me—thank you for helping me find a home in Chambana and in writing. I have learned so much from you.

To my friends and colleagues at the University of Utah, especially: Allie Field Bell, Stephanie Choi, Diana Clarke, Matty Layne Glasgow, Chengru He, Kaitlin Hoelzer, Jasmine Khaliq, Jesse Kohn, Emad Jabini, Aristotle Johns, Hunter Lewinski, Corley Miller, Michelle Macfarlane, Ali Myers, Erin O'Luanaigh, Nick Pierce, Max Schleicher, Jamie Smith, Sam Thilén, Daniel Uncapher, Lindsey Webb, Isaac Willis, Jake Yordy, and Brandon Young. Thank you for your bigheartedness, care, and close attention—for spending time with this manuscript and so much of my other work. This book and these poems are so much better for it. I am a better writer and thinker for knowing you and your work.

To Camille Dungy and Mark Wunderlich, who offered gracious and incisive feedback on poems from this manuscript as visiting writers at the University of Utah: thank you for your sharp eyes and invaluable advice.

To the incredible mentors and teachers I've had over the years, especially: Amy Quan Barry, Scott Black, Sean Bishop, Corey Butters, Vince Cheng, Kate Coles, Katharina Gerstenberger, Janice N. Harrington, Amy Jaeger-Raml, Anne Jamison, Doug Kearney, Christopher Kempf, Ron Kuka, Katie Lanning, Mike Madonick, Vicki Mahaffey, Judith Claire Mitchell, Kim Moreland, Ann Muellenbach, Sarah Oftedahl, Jackie Osherow, Paisley Rekdal, Ken Ristow, Kay Robbins, Maeera Shreiber, Jodee Stanley, D. J. Thielke, and David Zimmerman. Deepest thanks for your guidance, generosity, and wisdom— I will never stop being grateful.

To Corey Van Landingham, my MFA final project adviser, who believed in these poems from the very beginning and helped me shape them into this book: thank you so much for all your time and care. Thank you for both your untiring mentorship and steadfast support of me and my work—this book would not exist without you.

Profound gratitude to my beloved friends, near and far: Bree Bennett, Max Carroll, Maddie Davidsen, Paul Davidson, Danielle Fortin, Kris Harmelink, Zoë Hill, Taylor Hoffman, Kelsey Marten, Katie Miller, Gabe Resch, Alix Walters, Alonzoeh Stone, Emma Wichman, and Karl Wichman. Your friendship, love, humor, and inspired creativity have kept me alive and given me hope.

And finally, to my family—your love and support have meant everything to me. Thank you.

# Notes

1. "Courtesy and Horror" is after "Unspeakable" by Sharon Olds, its title originating in the lines: "He shows no anger, / I show no anger but in flashes of humor, / all is courtesy and horror."

2. The title of "Fire and Powder" comes from *Romeo and Juliet*, act 2, scene 6, verses 9–11: "These violent delights have violent ends, / And in their triumph die; like fire and powder, / Which as they kiss consume."

3. Apparat's "Goodbye," the main title/theme for the opening credits of the television show *Dark*, is an example of a piece in D♭ Minor, an uncommon musical key.

4. *Damnatio memoriae*, a Latin phrase meaning "condemnation of memory," refers to the practice of scrubbing a deceased person, often a former ruler, from history. It was a judgment that could be passed by the Roman Senate on traitors who brought dishonor to the Roman state. Examples of *damnatio* range from the destruction of statues and currency bearing the image of the deceased to the erasure or rewriting of official documents.

5. HMS *Erebus* and HMS *Terror* are the names of the two ships lost along with all hands in Sir Captain John Franklin's failed 1845 expedition to find the Northwest Passage. *Erebus* (or *Erebos*, from the Greek Ἔρεβος, meaning "deep darkness, shadow" or "covered") was named for the deep darkness at the entrance to Hades in Greek mythology. The wreck of *Erebus* was finally discovered in 2014, *Terror* in 2016.

6. "Waltz No. 2" is after Dmitri Shostakovich's "The Second Waltz, Op. 99a."

Printed in the United States
by Baker & Taylor Publisher Services